Title page A US LVTP 7
amphibious fighting
vehicle.

Endpapers A camouflaged
Leopard 1 accompanies
Canadian infantrymen into
attack.

This book was devised and produced by
Multimedia Publications (UK) Ltd

Editor: Jeff Groman
Design: John Strange and Associates
Picture Research: Military Archive &
Research Services – John & Diane Moore.
Production: Arnon Orbach

Copyright © Multimedia Publications
(UK) Ltd 1984

ISBN 1 85106 010 3

A Kola Book

Originated by D. S. Colour International Ltd,
London.
Printed by Cayfosa, Barcelona, Spain
Dep. Leg. B-35514 - 1984

Charles Messenger

A KOLA BOOK

CONTENTS

Introduction

It was just under seventy years ago, after the outbreak of World War I, that the tank made its first appearance on the battlefield. It did so in an effort to break the deadlock of trench warfare in France, which had been brought about by the advent of the machine gun, the magazine rifle and the quick-firing artillery gun. It did not immediately succeed in doing this, for the first tanks were too primitive in design. However, the seeds were sown, and by November 1918, when World War I ended, the potential of the tank had been realized.

The era of Blitzkrieg

During the next twenty years many nations experimented with tanks, but it was only the Germans who really appreciated the effect that they could have, if properly handled. The result was their Blitzkrieg or 'lightning war' campaigns of 1939-42 which changed the face of Europe.

The Allies soon learnt the lesson, and the tank dominated all theaters of World War II, apart from the jungles of the Pacific Islands and Burma. Both sides soon realized that, for the tank to be decisive on the battlefield, it still needed help from other sections of the army, especially the infantry and artillery. Yet these had to be able to keep up with the tank, and hence other types of armored fighting vehicle were quickly developed, including Infantry Combat Vehicles and Self-propelled Artillery.

Modern warfare

Since 1945 armored vehicles have remained a cornerstone of national armories, and there have been few conflicts in which they have not made an appearance. They have fought in major wars such as those between Israel and the Arab States, and in Vietnam; and they have equally served in counter-insurgency operations such as those in Northern Ireland and Afghanistan.

New threats to the tank have been developed, especially the anti-tank guided missile used by infantry, as in the 1973 Yom Kippur War, and mounted in helicopters, as used against North Vietnamese armor in 1972. These have caused some people to conclude that the day of the tank is almost over. This is not so: if anything,

the tank is still as dominant as ever. This is particularly so in Europe, where World War III, if it ever came, would be mainly fought on land. The Soviets rely very heavily on armor to achieve quick victory, while the West places just as much emphasis on it in order to deny this to the Soviets.

What must be emphasized is that the tank on its own is not a decisive weapon in any battle. There are many different types of armored vehicle, and it is these operating together in the right mix, along with other weapon systems, which produce the recipe for victory in the land battle.

Limitations of the tank

Although tanks are powerful weapons, they do have their limitations. Their size makes them easy to spot in the open, and so they will spend much time hiding in woods until they have to come into action. They are noisy, which means that they can be quickly detected, and their sound recognized, even in darkness. They are very vulnerable to attack by infantrymen with hand-held anti-tank weapons in villages and woods, and therefore need to have friendly infantry with them.

They also need frequent resupply of fuel and ammunition, and constant maintenance to keep them working. Their heavy weight also restricts their mobility, especially where the terrain is boggy and bridges are light. Every commander must, when employing a force of tanks, be aware of these limitations if he is to get the best use out of them.

Tanks of the future

Many experts now believe that the tank has already reached its greatest weight and size, and that future generations of tanks can only get smaller. The main reason lies in the latest form of anti-tank weapons. Called Precision Guided Munitions, these enable aircraft, helicopters, artillery and mortars to engage and destroy tanks very much more effectively than up to now.

These munitions are either laser-guided or are heat-seeking, and as they come into service the threats against the tank are certainly multiplying. The tank of the future is therefore likely to weigh less than 40 tons compared with its present minimum of 50 tons, and will have no turret, with the crew all in the hull. They may either have just a gun mounted above the hull, or nothing at all, the gun being situated inside the hull, and raised above it only when in action. It will be loaded automatically rather than by one of the crew, and the crew will be reduced to three or even two men. The future tank may not be very conspicuous on the battlefield, but when it is used its effect will be just as decisive as it has always been.

Challengers, Britain's latest main battle tank, advance. If near to the enemy, tanks always move at top speed and are covered by other tanks from static positions.

CHAPTER 1
Master Weapon of War

The tank is essentially a mobile gun platform, whose tasks on the battlefield are the destruction of enemy armored vehicles, providing close support to friendly infantry and, above all, shock action. This is making maximum use of its characteristics of impressive firepower, armored protection, mobility and the flexibility provided by having good radio communications to hit the enemy hard at the critical moment in the battle.

Devastating firepower

All tank producing nations agree that firepower is the most important characteristic. Over the years tank guns have increased in size and the most popular is now the 120mm caliber tank gun. This, together with today's sophisticated fire control systems, enables the tank to hit enemy armored vehicles and destroy them out to ranges of over 3000 yards.

Up until recently the barrel was always rifled (lined with a spiral groove). This gave maximum accuracy by imparting spin to the projectile. A problem with this is that the rifling wears very quickly, making the gun inaccurate. Now, however, many nations have adopted the smoothbore gun. This enables hotter charges to be used, which will send the projectile further, and the problem of inaccuracy has been overcome by giving the projectile fins so that it flies through the air like a dart. This is called fin stabilization.

Modern shells

The tank gun uses two types of ammunition: Kinetic Energy ammunition, which relies on speed and mass to penetrate armor, and Chemical Energy ammunition, where the speed of the round flying through the air does not matter as much as the chemical effect when it hits the target. Kinetic Energy projectiles look like darts when they leave the gun muzzle, and are made of very hard metal. The thicker or more sloped the armor, the less chance they have to penetrate.

With Chemical Energy rounds, it does not matter how thick or sloped the armor is. One type is called High Explosive Squashhead. This has a soft

Chieftain, which has been in British service since 1967 and is likely to continue to be so for a number of years. This one is mounting simulated firing equipment for use in training and the orange smoke indicates that it has been hit.

Below The crew of a US M551 Sheridan mount up. Designed as a reconnaissance tank, it is unique in that its 152mm gun fires both the Shillelagh anti-tank guided missile and a conventional HEAT round.

Far Right The Swedish Strv 103 or S Tank. Unlike other main battle tanks, it has no turret and has to turn on its tracks to traverse the gun. Its advantage is its low height, making a small target for the enemy. Tanks of the future may follow a similar concept.

Right Unlike most tanks, the S Tank is light enough to swim under its own power, being propelled by its tracks and using a flotation screen to give it buoyancy.

metal nose, is filled with explosive and has a base fuze. When it hits an enemy tank it 'cowpats' on the armor and the fuze detonates the explosive: this sends shock waves through the armor, causing pieces of it to break off on the inside and fly around the turret and hull.

The other type of Chemical Energy round is the High Explosive Anti-tank or Hollow Charge round. This has an inverted cone-shaped hollow in the front, which is lined with metal and has explosive in the rear. When it hits the target it detonates and sends a thin jet of molten metal through the armor. To guard against Chemical Energy attack, spaced armor – two thicknesses of armor with a space in between – and laminated armor, made up of a sandwich of different materials, are used. Hollow Charge warheads are also used in anti-tank guided missiles.

Ten seconds to strike

However good the gun and ammunition, unless targets can be identified and destroyed quickly the tank is of little use on the battlefield. The equipment used to spot the target and lay the gun accurately on it is called the fire control system. Nowadays, this is very sophisticated and is made up of the commander's and gunner's sights, a laser rangefinder and a computer. The computer contains ballistic information on the path the projectile takes through the air at various ranges, and will tell the gunner which part of his sight to lay on the target. Modern fire control systems mean that a tank crew now has a very good chance of spotting and hitting an enemy tank all within ten seconds. The crew also have special sights for use by night and so the tank is able to fight 'round the clock'.

The main battle tank of today weighs 50-60 tons. It therefore needs a very powerful engine, especially to enable it to travel at speeds of up to 40 mph. In the old days petrol engines were used, but these have now been

Left Note how the gun barrel on this Chieftain has been camouflaged to break up its outline.

Bottom Left A Soviet T-54 tank. This was the main Soviet tank of the 1950s, but is still in service, although its 100mm rifled gun is little match for modern main battle tanks.

Below US M60 in winter conditions.

replaced by diesel engines because they are less likely to catch fire, and they also have a better fuel consumption. Even so, a modern tank has a range of little more than 200 miles on a full tank, and this will be even less if it is doing much cross-country work. Tanks use automatic gearboxes, which make them simple to drive and, with several reverse gears, can travel as fast backwards as they can forwards. This is very important if a tank is caught in the open and wants to get behind cover quickly.

Fighting crew

Most tanks have a crew of four. In the turret are the commander, who is in charge, the gunner and the loader, who also operates the radios. The driver is the one member in the hull. Some tanks, however, especially Soviet ones, have replaced the loader by a machine, the autoloader, which means that the turret does not have to be so large. The crew will normally fight from inside the tank with the hatches closed, especially if there is a threat of chemical or nuclear weapons being used. The interior can be sealed and pure air passed through a filter, which is normally mounted at the rear of the turret.

M551 Sheridan firing the Shillelagh missile.

Left The US M60A1, mounting a dozer blade, which is used for improving fire positions, on exercise in Germany. This mounts a 105mm rifled gun, and is gradually being replaced by the M1 Abrams.

Bottom Left The newest US tank is the M1 Abrams. These early models mount the 105mm rifled gun, but later ones will have a 120mm smoothbore.

Right The Soviet T-80. This is essentially a T-72, but with an improved fire control system and better armor. It can be identified by the smoke grenade dischargers, used to provide a local smokescreen for protection, mounted on the turret front on either side of the main armament.

A fine shot of a Chieftain. Its 120mm rifled gun is still one of the most powerful in the world, and is used in Challenger.

Left US M1 Abrams on an approach march somewhere in Germany. Note how the crew's equipment is strapped onto the turret.

Below Left A British Challenger undergoing mobility tests.

Below The Italian OF-40, which is in service with the United Arab Emirates, firing its 105mm gun. The box above the gun is an armored searchlight for use with white light or infrared.

Bottom The Israeli Merkava, designed after much desert tank fighting experience. It is unusual in having the engine in the front, and a stowage compartment in the rear for extra ammunition or for carrying infantry.

Left A West German Leopard 2 firing on the range.

Below Left Tanks require much maintenance to keep them fit for battle. Here a Chieftain gets a new power pack.

Below Chieftains night firing. They use infrared searchlights to identify their targets.

CHAPTER TWO
Eyes and Ears of the Army

No commander can expect to fight a battle and win it unless he has a good idea of what the enemy are doing. In this age of satellites and spy planes, it is easy to forget that there is still a very real need for effective reconnaissance on the ground, and much of this is provided by the armored reconnaissance vehicle.

When the enemy is advancing, reconnaissance troops monitor his movements in order to recognize the main lines of his thrust, so that defenses can be deployed accordingly. When one's own side is advancing, the task of reconnaissance troops is to probe the enemy's defenses to try and find weak spots, so that the main attack can be launched with the best possible chance of success.

The armored reconnaissance vehicle

There are two types of reconnaissance. Reconnaissance by fire is firing at the enemy position to persuade him to shoot back, thus giving away details of his position and equipment. The danger with this is that the reconnaissance vehicle might be destroyed before it can send back the information it has gained, and hence reconnaissance by stealth is preferred. This means getting into a position where the enemy can be seen, but cannot spot the reconnaissance vehicle. To do this, the vehicle needs to be small, but there are differing opinions on whether it should be propelled by wheels or tracks.

Wheeled vehicles have two major advantages over tracked ones. They are much quieter and are easier to maintain. Tracked vehicles, however, have a much better cross-country performance and can traverse terrain which is impossible for a wheeled vehicle. On the other hand, wheeled vehicles are generally cheaper to produce, which is a major reason why many armies, especially those of Third World countries, prefer them.

Guns for the job

There is also a constant debate on what type of armament a

The latest US reconnaissance vehicle – M3 Bradley, with a crew of five, 25mm cannon and twin TOW antitank guided missile launchers.

reconnaissance vehicle should have. If it is to see without being seen, there is a good argument for making it very lightly armed, with just a machine gun, for this helps to keep its overall size small. Yet there are times when it will be forced to fight for information, and a machine gun is of little use when confronted with another armored vehicle.

Some designers therefore opt for a 20-30mm cannon, which is effective against light armored vehicles, but not so against main battle tanks. Others argue that, because a reconnaissance vehicle is of little use unless it can survive long enough to get information gained on the enemy back to headquarters, it should be able to engage a tank if necessary. This can be done by mounting either a gun with caliber ranging from 76-105mm, or an anti-tank guided weapon system.

Endurance is all

Vehicle size also dictates the number of crewmen a reconnaissance car can carry. The minimum is two, one to drive and the other to command and observe. This keeps the vehicle small, but can be very tiring for the crew. They will often be expected to operate without respite for days at a time, and lack of rest will mean that the efficiency of the 2-man crew will fall off very quickly. Many reconnaissance vehicles therefore have a crew of three – commander, gunner and driver. Often, though, reconnaissance troops will be expected to perform additional tasks such as preparing booby traps or laying mines, and so some vehicles have as many as five crewmen.

Instruments of vision

The reconnaissance vehicle's surveillance aids are its most important asset. In their simplest form these are the eyes and ears of the crew members. Certainly, when in a static position, the crew will often dismount, leave their vehicle behind cover and set up an observation post,

Top Left British 76mm Scorpion tracked reconnaissance vehicle in the Arabian desert.

Above The French AMX-13 light tank with its oscillating turret equipped with an autoloader. This turret is used on many other hulls.

Far Left The French Panhard ERC90 Sagaie on parade with the Mexican Army, who call it Lynx.

23

Right Many countries use the US Commando, which appears in a number of configurations. This V-150 version has twin 7.62mm machine guns and can carry up to 12 men.

Below The Swiss Mowag Shark firing its 105mm gun. There are also 4 and 6 wheel variants, some of which are used by the Canadian Army and US Marine Corps.

Below Right This Mowag 4-wheel variant is called Spy and mounts a 12.7mm machine gun.

running a telephone cable back to the vehicle radios.

Besides the human element, the vehicle's own vision aids are very important. A reconnaissance car is equipped with sights like those on a tank, with very good magnification; and its crew are able to see at night or in poor visibility, using infra-red or image intensification techniques. Some vehicles also mount radars, which are a very useful surveillance aid. Others have specialist roles, with devices which can monitor nuclear radiation or the presence of chemical agents.

Ground reconnaissance is the eyes of an army, and the skill with which it is carried out can make the difference between defeat and victory. The reconnaissance vehicle must be tailored to carry out its task but, in the event, it will only be as good as its crew. To be a good scout requires a mixture of quick wittedness, initiative and low cunning, as well as a clear understanding of the strengths and limitations of the reconnaissance vehicle and its equipment.

The West German Luchs armored car. Unlike most wheeled vehicles, it has not just all-wheel drive, but all-wheel steering as well.

Below The 90mm gunned Brazilian EE-9 Cascavel. The splashboard in the front prevents water entering the driver's compartment when swimming.

Right A French Army Panhard ERC90 Sagaie crew prepare to leave barracks.

Below Right The French AML90, with 90mm gun. Several different turrets with varying armament can be mounted on this hull.

Left M3 Bradley fires a TOW missile.

Below A Scorpion changing position. Many crewmen wear 'bone domes' to protect them when going at speed over rough terrain.

Top Left Another French armored car is the AMX-10RC, which has a 105mm gun and is in French and Moroccan Army service.

Left A British Fox, with 30mm Rarden gun, watches for the enemy.

Above This British Scorpion crew are manning an observation post. The gunner is on the right and the commander on the left.

Below British Army Scorpions on an operational patrol in Belize.

CHAPTER 3
Carrying the Infantry

On the mechanized battlefield of today infantry and tanks work very closely with one another. The infantryman must therefore be able to keep up with armor, and hence needs armored vehicles to carry him. He could, of course, ride on the back of the tank, but this is very unsatisfactory as he is very vulnerable to enemy fire and, in any event, would hinder the fighting activity of the tank. Instead he has two types of specially designed vehicles: the Armored Personnel Carrier and the Mechanized Infantry Combat Vehicle (or Infantry Fighting Vehicle).

Battlefield transport

The Armored Personnel Carrier to the infantryman on the battlefield is just like the cab to the man in the street. It takes him to where he wants to go, drops him off, and then goes to the rear and waits for him to call for it again. This is particularly so in defense, where the infantry's task is to hold ground, which they will do dug in and on their feet. In the attack it will take him close to his objective before he dismounts and sometimes, if the opposition is weak, will take him right onto it, which increases the speed and momentum of the attack. It is also the infantryman's mobile home and will store any equipment which he does not immediately require for the particular task in hand.

Each Armored Personnel Carrier can carry a squad of infantry – that is, 6-9 men. Remaining permanently with the vehicle are the commander and driver. It is normally armed with just a machine gun, but some models also have weapons slits in the side of the hull to enable the infantry to fire when inside – usually when attacking, although the fire is not very accurate.

Its protective armor is not as tough as that of a main battle tank, being designed merely to keep out shell splinters and small arms fire. Some models of Armored Personnel Carrier have collective nuclear and chemical protection in the same way as a tank, but others do not. In any event, once the infantry open the door at the rear to dismount, this collective protection is lost and the occupants have to rely

The Alvis Spartan Armored Personnel Carrier, a member of the Scorpion family. In the British Army it is not used to carry infantry, but has a number of specialized roles.

Left No less than fifty countries use the US M113 APC, which has a crew of two and can carry 11 infantrymen.

Right A wheeled APC is the French Panhard VCR, which in its basic version shown here mounts a 20mm cannon.

on their own protective suits and respirators.

In some cases the basic carrier is adapted to carry the infantryman's heavier weapons. Thus there are mortar carriers, from which a mortar can be fired through the roof hatch; recoilless anti-tank gun carriers; and anti-tank guided weapons carriers.

A mobile fortress

The Infantry Fighting Vehicle, as its name suggests, is more than a battlefield cab; it is a vehicle from which to fight. Unlike the Armored Personnel Carrier it has a recognizable turret with either a 20-30mm cannon or sometimes a medium caliber gun. A number of versions also incorporate anti-tank guided weapons systems as well as the cannon or gun. This armament is designed to engage light armored vehicles rather than main battle tanks: heavy tanks alongside are normally assigned to tackle enemy tanks.

At the same time, this type of vehicle is also a personnel carrier as well and, because it is a fighting vehicle, will remain much closer to the infantry when they have dismounted. However, once the infantry have established themselves in a position on the ground, they do not like to have their Infantry Fighting Vehicle standing too close beside them, for it may be seen and could draw artillery fire. It is therefore usually deployed some distance to one side. In terms of protection, the Infantry Fighting

Left The AT105 Saxon has just entered British Army service. Wheeled AFVs are often used for internal security.

Below Left The British Army's MCV-80 with 30mm Rarden gun will shortly enter service as an infantry combat vehicle.

Vehicle has the same strength of armor as the personnel carrier, but its more sophisticated weapons systems make it a more expensive vehicle.

Wheels or tracks?

While the majority of Armored Personnel Carriers and Infantry Fighting Vehicles are tracked, some are on wheels. Apart from being less costly, wheeled infantry armored vehicles are very much better suited to internal security roles – riot control, for example, or controling urban terrorists. Most people tend to think of any armored vehicle on tracks as being a tank, and this can be of great propaganda value to the terrorist or insurgent. Internal security versions are often fitted with special-to-role items such as water cannon; fenders to ward off petrol bomb attacks; and plows for clearing improved roadblocks.

Two inherent dangers

The infantry's armored vehicles enable infantrymen to continue to play a major role in the land battle of today by giving them the ability to move about the battlefield under fire. There are, however, two drawbacks. In some ways these vehicles have made the infantry a more recognizable target than they were before. If the vehicle is hit while the infantry are not inside, they are immediately robbed of their mobility and can play little part in the fast moving armor battle. If they are inside, then it is not just the vehicle which is lost but the infantry also.

The other drawback is that the more heavily armed the vehicle, the more infantrymen have to stay on board as members of the permanent crew, and the fewer there will be to jump out of the back and carry out their vital dismounted tasks.

Above The Brazilian EE-11 Urutu requires little preparation for swimming, and uses its tracks and hydrojets to give it a top speed of 6 knots in water.

Far Right An M2 Bradley being put through its paces. Very similar to the M3, it carries a total of ten men and has firing ports in the hull sides and rear.

Right The West German Marder Mechanized Infantry Combat Vehicle, which has a 20mm cannon. It has a crew of four and carries six infantrymen.

Left Many Third World countries prefer wheeled AFVs because they are cheaper and easier to maintain. These Swiss Mowag Rolands are in Sierra Leonean service.

Below Left The US FMC MICV was not taken up by the US Army but is used by the Dutch, Belgian and Philippine Armies.

Below APCs and other light AFVs can be lifted by helicopter, which is a quick way of recovering those which have broken down. Here a US Chinook in RAF colors lifts an Alvis Stormer, which is similar to Spartan, but with an additional set of road wheels.

Above The British Army's FV432 APC has been in service for over 20 years. Some will be replaced by MCV-80, but others are likely to run on for some time to come.

Right APCs also often carry infantry heavy weapons. Here a Dutch crew set up their 120mm mortar, having dismounted from their DAF YP408 wheeled APC.

Above Right The French Creusot-Loire/Saviem VAB wheeled APC carries ten infantrymen and is used by a number of African and Middle Eastern countries.

CHAPTER 4
Modern Artillery

The motto of the British Royal Regiment of Artillery is *Ubique,* which means 'Everywhere'. This is a very apt description of artillery, without whose ability to lay down quick and accurate supporting fire battles could not be won. Traditionally, artillery guns have always been mounted on wheels, drawn at first by horses and later by wheeled vehicles. This is called 'towed' artillery and much still exists, although it is normally deployed in more difficult terrain, such as jungle, mountains and marsh, which is not suitable for armored vehicles.

There is, however, little place for it on today's fast-moving mechanized battlefield because it is too vulnerable to enemy fire and needs, like the infantry, to be able to keep up with the tank. Hence, modern artillery has been put on tracks, given some armor protection and the means to propel itself without the help of a towing vehicle. This is known as self-propelled artillery.

Long-range fire

At first sight there seems to be little difference between a tank and a self-propelled artillery gun. Both are on tracks; both have a gun, usually in a turret; and the turret can turn right round in a complete circle. The essential difference is that of role. While tanks are designed to engage other armored vehicles that they can see to aim at (this is called direct fire), artillery fires at targets at up to ten times the range of a tank, and ones which the gun crew cannot see themselves.

To do this, the artillery crew relies on a forward observer to give the necessary target details and to direct the aim of fire. The term for this is indirect fire, and it is designed to lay down a heavy concentration of explosive over an area rather than a point target. For this, the artillery gun requires different sighting devices and a much higher gun elevation in order to be able to fire the shell over the longer ranges. Because it is always positioned behind the front line it is not under such a serious threat from enemy tanks, and hence it is given somewhat lighter armor.

A 155mm self-propelled howitzer turret mounted on A Vickers Mk 3 tank chassis. This is a good way of getting further use out of obsolete tanks.

Right Ammunition resupply is a major problem for artillery, especially when under fire. The US Field Artillery Ammunition Supply Vehicle, here replenishing an M110 8in howitzer, is one answer.

Below Artillery ammunition is heavy. This US M109 155mm round weighs over 90lbs and mechanical assistance is needed to load it into the breech.

Far Right Here is the Soviet M1974 122mm SP howitzer.

Below Right The US M109 SP gun is used by many NATO armies.

More men on board

The artillery gun is also likely to fire for a longer period of time than a tank, and ammunition expenditure will be very much higher. Only a limited number of rounds can actually be carried on the gun itself, and so the balance is in a separate vehicle, which stays close to the gun at all times. By the same token, in order to keep up a prolonged rate of fire the gun needs a much larger crew than that of a tank. On average this is normally 5-6 men. This includes the commander, the driver, the gun layer, the loader and the ammunition handlers who prepare the rounds for firing.

The shells

The most common type of ammunition used by the artillery gun is the High Explosive round, which is ideal for destroying trench systems or infantry on their feet in the open, and can also make life unpleasant for armored fighting vehicles. The fuze on it can be set for the round to burst in the air or on impact with the ground. Smoke rounds are also used frequently to conceal the movement of friendly armor and infantry, and by night the battlefield can be lit up with illuminating rounds. The gun will have a few anti-tank rounds, but will only fire these as a last resort in the event of a sudden enemy breakthrough.

Keeping up with the battle

The key to the effectiveness of artillery on the battlefield is quick response – the ability to bring down accurate fire, on request by armor and infantry, at a moment's notice. To do

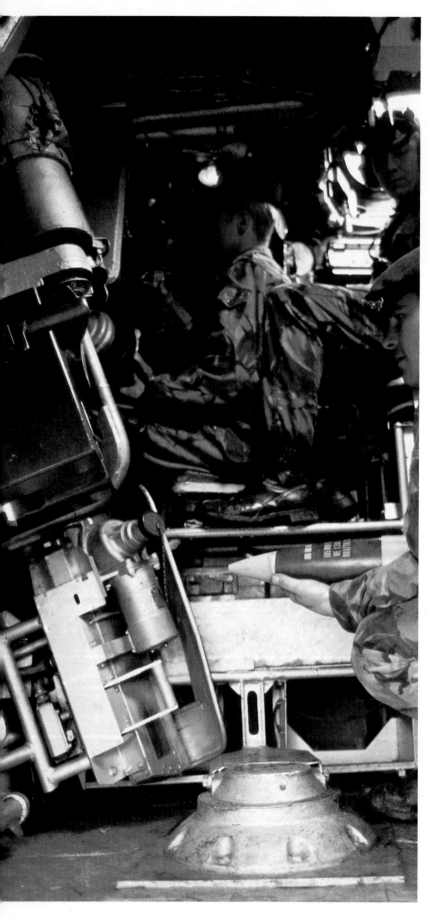

this it works on the principle of 'always having a leg on the ground', however fluid the battle. It is organized into batteries of 6-8 guns, and while one battery moves position – and these moves are frequent, not just because of a fast moving battle but also to prevent the enemy locating the guns and bringing down fire on them – another is static and ready to fire. This is where self-propelled artillery shows its marked advantage over towed guns: it can be brought into action more quickly, and hence can keep up with the fast tempo of mobile warfare.

A vital service
Artillery is vitally important, but the advent of Precision Guided Munitions is about to make it even more so, for these will confer upon it an altogether new role – that of an anti-armor weapon. Another revolutionary new role will be to lay minefields, by firing shells containing anti-tank mine submunitions. The ability to lay instant minefields qualifies self-propelled artillery still better to keep pace with the fast-moving battle of modern warfare. The complaint is often heard today that there is never enough artillery available on the battlefield. It is a cry which is likely to become louder in the future.

Left The interior of the British 105mm Abbot SP gun. At the top is the gun commander, to his right the gun layer, and below the loader.

Top Right The British Abbot firing on the range. It uses the FV432 APC chassis and a 105mm gun.

Right Carrying out nuclear/chemical decontamination on an 8 inch M110 SP gun. This fires both nuclear and conventional rounds.

Far Left The French AMX 155mm GCT SP gun, which is in service with France, Iraq and Saudi Arabia.

Below Left The Japanese Type 74 105mm SP howitzer. The Japanese also have the more powerful Type 75 155mm.

Left The German JPz Kanone, here in Belgian service, is not an SP artillery gun but a tank destroyer.

Below SP guns do not have to have a turret as these French 155mm Mk F3 howitzers show.

CHAPTER 5
Specialized Armor

So far we have covered the basic members of the family of armor. There are, however, more specialist armored vehicles in service in the armies of today. Although these are often not in the forefront of the stage, the tasks which they perform are nonetheless important.

Air-raid defense

The air threat, both from fixed and rotary wing aircraft, is something which constantly worries ground force commanders since modern air-delivered munitions are very destructive. Most armored vehicles have a machine gun mounted on top which is used in the air defense role, but its range is very limited and it is no match for a fast-flying jet. To provide additional cover, there is now an increasing range of specialist air defense armored vehicles. Many of these mount quick-firing cannon, and incorporate radar, which can locate targets out to ten miles. These are then tracked and the guns will automatically lock on to the aircraft, engaging it when it closes to about two miles. Some surface-to-air missile systems are also mounted on armor chassis.

Engineers

Another range of specialist vehicles are those which are used for engineer tasks. The role of engineers in war is to impede the enemy's mobility, while enhancing that of their own side. The best way to achieve the former is through minefields, and a number of basic types of armored vehicle have been adapted as minefield layers. Usually these are Armored Personnel Carriers, which have plenty of room inside to carry mines. Tank chassis are also used as bridge-layers to enable armor to cross streams and anti-tank ditches. Others have a special 165mm gun mounted in the turret. This is very effective against concrete emplacements. There are also plows which can be fitted to tanks for clearing minefields. Finally, there are a number of vehicles fitted with dozer blades and winches, and which are built specially for engineer

The West German Gepard low level air defense vehicle in action. Its radar can acquire aircraft up to five miles range and the twin 35mm cannon have an effective range of some two miles.

Center The French Thomson-CSF Sabre air defense turret mounted on a British Chieftain hull.

Below Another of the Swiss Mowag family, the 6 x 6 Piranha, here equipped with a ground surveillance radar.

Far Right The British Ranger antipersonnel mine delivery system mounted on the FV432.

reconnaissance tasks. These are usually able to 'swim' as well.

The commander in the field

Armored Command Vehicles are also widely used. These are basically Armored Personnel Carriers, but often with the roof raised to provide more room inside. Fitted with mapboards and additional radios, they are used at most levels of command. Their advantage is that they do give commanders and their staffs protection against enemy artillery fire. Also, like artillery, headquarters do not like to stay too long in one place, in case they are located by the enemy, and if equipped with armored vehicles they can pack up and move quickly.

Saving the wounded

Many logistics vehicles are also armored. Ambulances, again usually based on Armored Personnel Carriers but with stretchers fitted inside, need to go right forward to rescue wounded men on the battlefield. Then there are repair and recovery vehicles which again have to go up to the front line to attend to vehicle casualties. Many of

these are also based on a tank chassis, which has the power to tow disabled tanks. Some artillery ammunition carriers, too, are armored.

The amphibians
One final category is that of the armored amphibious vehicles. Most light armored vehicles are able to 'swim', often with little preparation; and they are propelled by their wheels or tracks through the water. Main battle tanks are too heavy to do this, although Soviet tanks have snorkeling equipment so that they can traverse river bottoms. This is, however, risky and many things can go wrong. A number of armored vehicles are in use with marine forces that are specifically designed for amphibious landings. These have a much better performance in water than those whose primary function is on dry land.

Far Left The German MaK engineer vehicle on a Leopard I chassis. Designed for improving river bank entry/exits, it never went beyond prototype.

Below Left Chieftain Armored Recovery Vehicle.

Left Soviet ZSU-23-4 air defense vehicle, which has gained a high reputation for its effectiveness.

Below The British FV180 Combat Engineer Tractor. It is towing the Giant Viper mine clearance system which is based on an explosive hose.

Armor in its many forms

Many of these specialist vehicles are based on existing tanks, reconnaissance and infantry armored vehicles. Indeed, there are now whole families consisting of several different types, all derived from the same chassis and basic components. This is a much cheaper way of producing special-to-task vehicles than designing them from scratch, and makes maintenance and the supply of spare parts very much easier. What is striking, though, is the huge range of uses to which armored vehicles are put. In spite of the ever increasing threats to armor today more, rather than less, of these essential vehicles are likely to be seen on the battlefield of tomorrow.

Above Left British Centurion Beach Armored Recovery Vehicle.

Below Left The Brazilian EE-11 Urutu repair vehicle lifting a Urutu engine.

Above US Marine Corps LVTP 7s in Norway.

Below A Chieftain bridgelayer. The span of the bridge is over 80ft and it will take a main battle tank.

Above Some of the Combat Vehicle Reconnaissance (Tracked) family in British Army service – (left to right) Sultan (command), Spartan, Scorpion, Scimitar (30mm Rarden gun), Scorpion, Spartan, Samaritan (ambulance). Other members are Samson (recovery) and Striker (antitank missile).

Right The Dutch version of the German Gepard, recognizable by the different radar dish shape. It is called Cheetah.

Below The Franco-German Roland surface-to-air missile system in action.

Above The fully amphibious LVTP7 used by the US Marine Corps and by the Argentinians in their invasion of the Falkland Islands in 1982.

Left The French Panhard VCR mounting the HOT antitank missile launcher.

PICTURE ACKNOWLEDGEMENTS

Alvis (UK) Ltd. 31, 34-35, 43, 62-63 top **Engesa S.A.** 28, 40-41 top **FMC** title page, 20-21, 36-37, 41, 42 bottom, 63 center **Christopher F. Foss** endpapers, 16 bottom, 17, 22 top, 22-23, 32-33 top, 52, 53 top, 54-55, 60-61 bottom, 62 bottom, Mak Maschinenbau GmbH 58 top, Technische Handel MIJ 62 center **GNK Sankey** 38-39 **MacClancy Collection** 9, 12 bottom, 48 bottom left, 49 bottom **MARS** 24-25, 30, 49 top, 50, 59, Aeronutronic Ford 10-11, Armoured Division PR (Maile) 33 top, Creusot-Loire 53 bottom, R.G. Crossley 16 top, Crown Copyright 4-5, 14-15, 18 bottom, 44-45 top, 51 top, 58 bottom, DAF Eindhoven 44-45 bottom, Martin Horseman 60 top, Mowag 42 top, NATO 8 top, 12 top, Renault 45 bottom, Swedish Army 6 top, 7, Thomson CSF 56-57, US Army 6 bottom, 8 bottom, 18-19 **Mowag S.A.** 25 bottom, 56 left **Panhard-Levassor** 22 bottom, 29, 37 top, 63 bottom **Rex Features** 51 bottom, 61 top **Soldier Magazine** 2-3, 19 bottom, 33 bottom, 57 top, 61 bottom **Frank Spooner Pictures** front cover, back cover **Thyssen-Henschel** 26-27 **Vickers Ltd.** 46-47

Multimedia Publications (UK) Limited have endeavored to observe the legal requirements with regard to the rights of suppliers of photographic material.